# THE EVER-EVOLVING PARENT

## A Guide to Becoming a More Present Parent

### Nikki Janowiak

ISBN: 979-8-234-06550-6
First Edition: 2026
Published by Nikki Janowiak | Kalamazoo, Michigan

Medical & Professional Disclaimer:
The author of this guide is a certified TRTP™ practitioner, not a licensed physician, psychiatrist, or psychologist. The content provided is for educational and informational purposes only and is not intended as a substitute for professional medical advice, diagnosis, or treatment. Always seek the advice of your physician or other qualified health provider with any questions you may have regarding a medical or mental health condition.

Acknowledgments:
This work includes references and inspirations from the "Good Inside" philosophy by Dr. Becky Kennedy. The mantra "I am a good mom having a hard time" is a concept by Dr. Becky Kennedy and is used here with deep respect for her teachings and their impact on the conscious parenting community.

Printed in the United States of America

# Meet The Author
# Nikki Janowiak

Mother of two and certified TRTP™ Practitioner

After the birth of my second child, I found myself losing my shit every.single.day. After another moment of screaming at my child, I knew something needed to change. I started reading and learning, unlearning and becoming the person I now know and have grown to love and nurture.

I wanted to share my current biggest growth edges with other parents who are looking at their lives and wanting to be more present and regulated.

To the parents who are struggling on any level. I see you. I want you to know I still have my hard days. Through my evolution, I've learned that parenting will always have its "hard"; I just choose a different version of it now. I am no longer defined by my past reactions, but by my capacity to return to presence. These are the growth edges I have created in my life so that even on my hard days, I still have clarity and gratitude for this stage of life.

# A Note From One Parent to Another

I want to start out by stating I do not have a PhD in psychology, and I am not a doctor. I'm just a parent who had a really hard time finding herself in motherhood. To be honest, it didn't feel natural to me at all, and motherhood turned out to be something completely different than I had imagined.

For a long time, I was stuck in survival mode. This is what I call the "survival fog." Letting past patterns play out and dictate my future. Once I found my evolution, what I call the present ever-evolving stride. It became the most freeing feeling I have ever known.

That's why I created this guide: to help you create awareness in your life so you can find your own present, ever-evolving stride, too.

## Who is this guide for?

This is for the parent who's ready to create real, lasting change. This is for the one who may feel a bit lost in the daily grind and is looking for tools to help come back to the present moment.

My journey will look different than yours. I am sharing my growth edges to help spark awareness as you navigate yours.

You're not alone.
We are in this together.
By simply picking up this pocket guide, you have already started the work. You are already choosing awareness over the " survival fog."

**Great job!**

If these words speak to you, I know you're ready. Let's look at these growth edges together.

I have created this to be a quick read for a busy parent. For more details or a deeper conversation, I would love to hear from you!

**Email: Janowiaknikki@gmail.com**

**Instagram: @theeverevolvingmama**

Focus on my behavior before the kids behavior

What place am I parenting from right now

Get Curious focus on connection

It is safe for me to be present

I create my reality

Have I connected with myself today

# The Biggest Tool in My Toolbox
## Sticky Notes

At the start of my journey, you would have seen sticky notes everywhere in my house. My mirrors, my cabinets, by the TV, above the sink. They. Were. Everywhere.

The sticky notes you see throughout this guide are actual notes I used along my own journey. They are the exact "gifts" I gave myself to help me along my evolution.

**So why sticky notes?**
**I use them for two main reasons:**

**1. They are the ultimate pattern interrupters:**
I believe the first step to change is awareness. Once we have that awareness, our unconscious (subconscious) mind often does everything in its power to pull us back into what is familiar. It wants to keep us "safe" in old familiar loops, even if these patterns are no longer safe or serving us.

When I am rewiring an unhelpful thought pattern about myself, I read the new helpful sticky note and stop that old cycle in its tracks. Or when I find a new helpful parenting tool, I write it on a sticky note. This enables me to reach for the new tool.

These notes act as a "pattern interrupt." The sticky note tool helps me make the actual change. I keep that sticky note up until that new thought or behavior becomes who I am.

Think of these notes as the physical *pattern interrupt*. They help stop the old unhelpful pattern and give the mind and body a new direction to move in.

**Example:** My behavior of yelling at my kids. My unhelpful thought pattern used to be: "I am a bad mom." But after learning from one of my favorite psychologists, Dr. Becky Kennedy, my new helpful thought pattern is: "I am a good mom who had a hard moment."

**2. They are simple and fast:** When I am in a hard moment with my kids, or having unhelpful thoughts about myself, I don't have the time to open a self-help or parenting book or scroll through a course. I need the help now! Writing and reading these sticky notes throughout my day allows me to easily reach for my new tools, making them as effective as possible. I stop and look at the sticky note for guidance, and find my stride again. They are small bites of information that are easy to digest.

*I know you can do this. Trust the process. Trust yourself*

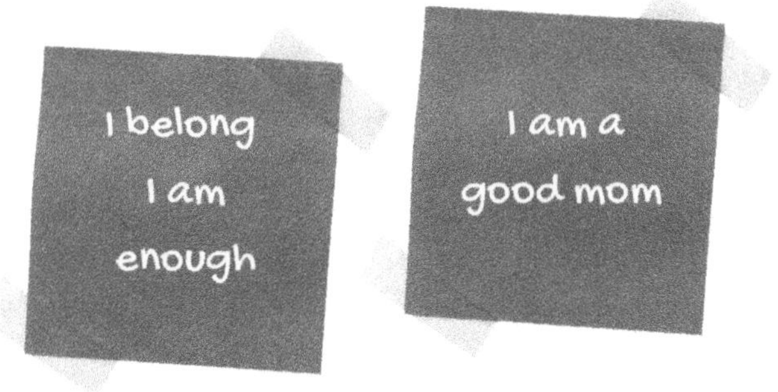

# HOW TO USE THIS GUIDE

While this information is a quick read, creating new neural pathways takes time. When a Growth Edge resonates with you, I encourage you to write it down on a sticky note and place it where you look the most.

This pocket guide is meant to create awareness in areas of your life where you desire to be more present.

Each Growth Edge shares a story of how it came to be in my life, a tool I use for staying present, and a "Level Up." The Level Up is meant to help spark awareness and guide you toward what is most sticky note worthy on your journey.

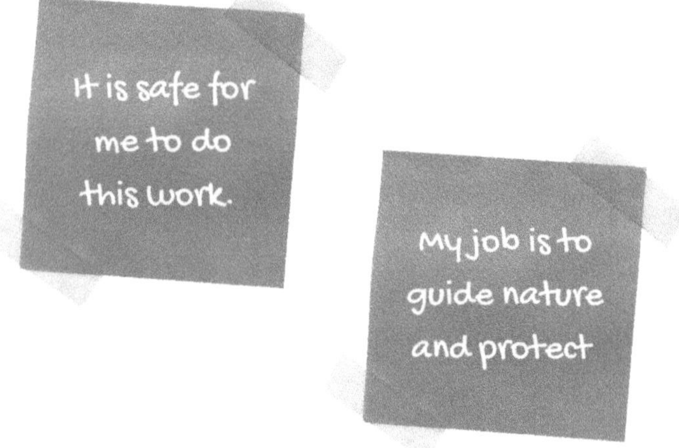

This space is saved for you. A landing pad for the sticky note tool. In the pages ahead, I'll share the actual sticky notes I have used to navigate my growth. By capturing what resonates on a sticky note or even a scrap piece of paper you can tape up later. The goal is to anchor that new awareness into our physical world by writing it down and placing it where you look most.

Depending on how this guide found its way into your hands, you may already find sticky notes tucked here, or you may find this space ready for your own. Place a small stack of blank sticky notes in the box below, or simply keep a favorite pen and paper handy so your tools are always within reach. Let this be your invitation to stay present, grab a note, and watch the evolution unfold. This doesn't have to be perfect, it just has to be yours.

Connection before correction

I am loved
I am safe
I can ground myself

My feelings will not overwhelm me

I create my reality

I am in control of my thoughts

It is safe for me to be in the moment

# Growth Edge 1
## I Am Responsible for My Own Healing

In my past, I would go to bed with a heavy feeling of shame. I was angry at my husband, frustrated with my kids, and just mad at the world around me. I thought the best place to start was by "fixing" my child's meltdowns, and assuming that would finally stop me from freaking out. (Woof! My logic at that time was a bit backwards.) I was pouring all my power and energy into the child in the room, and it was draining just to be me.

While reading a poster to my daughter about what we can control, it hit me: *this entire time, I have been trying to control everyone and everything around me.* I thought that if the world around me would just stop pissing me off, I would be "fixed."

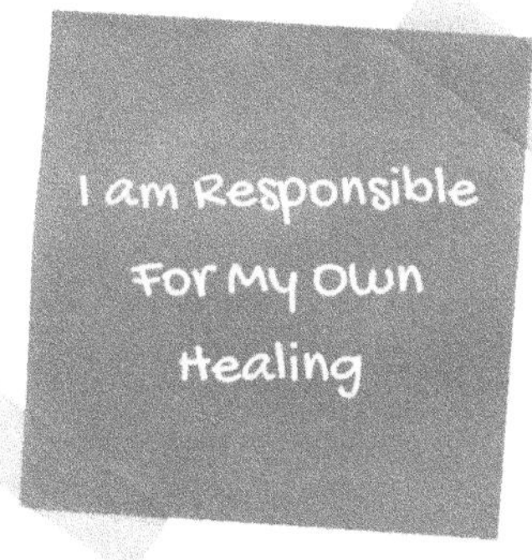

### The Shift: Focus on what you can control

In that moment, I realized I could only control *my* thoughts, *my* feelings, and *my* behaviors. The world around me wasn't responsible for *my* feelings. I was. The awareness that I only had the power to change my own actions was my starting point. Realizing that **I am responsible for my own healing was my growth edge.**

### My Tool: Grounding

When I notice myself trying to control things I have no power over, I recognize it as a signal that I've lost my center. I will go to the kitchen and re-read my current sticky notes to ground myself and refocus on the only thing I can control: my own regulation.

### The Level Up

I believe recognizing the urge to control things outside our power is a signal to connect within ourselves.

Are you giving your power to something you have no control over?

# GROWTH EDGE 2
## I HAD TO DO FOUNDATIONAL WORK

I started reading and listening to every parenting and self-help book and podcast I could find. I was gaining awareness of why I was reacting, but there was still a missing piece. My logic knew what to do, but my body and mind were still stuck in survival mode.

I couldn't logic my way into a new version of myself. I needed to do foundational work to help my nervous system find a sense of safety. Moving out of that constant survival fog opened up a level of clarity that was always within me. For the first time, I had access to it. It gave me the space to start choosing how I move through life, not just how I react to it.

### The Shift: Doing "the work" on ourselves is the greatest gift we can give our kids

Our families deserve a version of us that isn't constantly running on fumes or reacting from past pain. When we don't address our own "stuff," we often end up passing those same reactive patterns down to our children. I believe doing foundational work is about finding enough safety within ourselves. We all deserve a healthier version of ourselves, and so do our families.

### My Tool:  The Richards Trauma Process (TRTP™)

At this point, I realized my reactions were mainly coming from past pain, showing up in ways that didn't serve my family or me anymore. TRTP™ provided me with a framework to safely access the unconscious patterns that were driving my survival fog.  This became a catalyst for stepping into my ever-evolving journey. While this was the right fit for my foundational work, I encourage you to research and find a modality that resonates most with your journey.

### The Level Up

If you could respond from a place of internal safety instead of survival, how might that change the energy within you?

# Growth Edge 3
## I Am What I Consume

I will be the first to acknowledge that this growth edge is always evolving in my life.

For a long time, I was mindlessly scrolling social media, ignoring how food made my body feel, remaining oblivious to unhelpful thought patterns, and surrounding myself with toxic energy. Everything we fuel our minds and bodies with will eventually become who we are.

After doing the foundational work, I realized I had a choice to make: I could let aspects of my environment lead me back into survival mode, or I could intentionally step into the life I wanted to create.

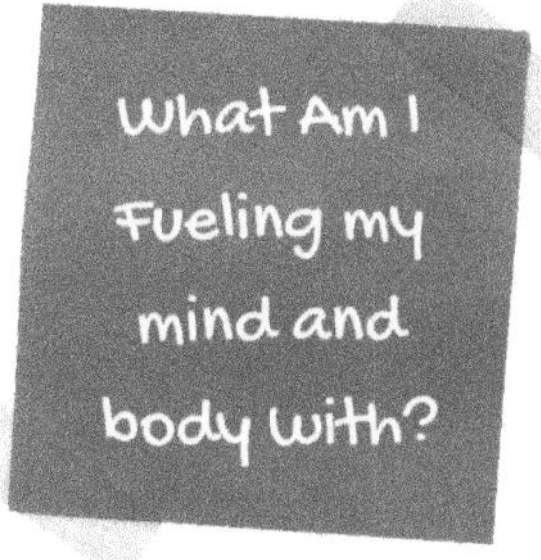

## The Shift: We have the power to create the environment around us

I made a conscious decision to become more present in my life. I started choosing to fuel my mind, my thoughts, and my body with things that lead to peace, not just more overwhelming noise.

When we stop feeding into the survival fog and start creating the life we want to live, that is power!

## My Tool: Capturing the Change

When I find something that I really want to embody, I add it to a sticky note. I look at the sticky note throughout the day and practice those new thoughts until they simply become a part of me.

Most of the accounts I follow and engage with online are voices aligned with my "Future Self." When I catch myself mindlessly scrolling, I make it 1% better by capturing what resonates and putting it on a sticky note! This helps me turn mindless scrolling into a great, ever-evolving parenting tool that I can bring into real life.

## The Level Up

Become deeply aware of what you consume. You have the power to choose what you let into your physical and mental space.

Are we fueling the survival fog or the evolution into a more present version of yourself?

# GROWTH EDGE 4
## SPIRAL STAIRCASE

At one point in my evolution,  I honestly thought I was just going in circles. I felt like I was failing. I kept coming back to these familiar struggles: myself, motherhood, marriage, career, friendships- and hitting a wall every time. I thought that once I "fixed" my morning routine, or finally "learned" to be more present, the struggles would just stop.

The truth is, life doesn't stop having hard moments.  The kids still have meltdowns, the schedule still gets messy, and there will always be tons of reasons to get pulled out of the moment. We can't wait for life to be perfect to start living in the now.

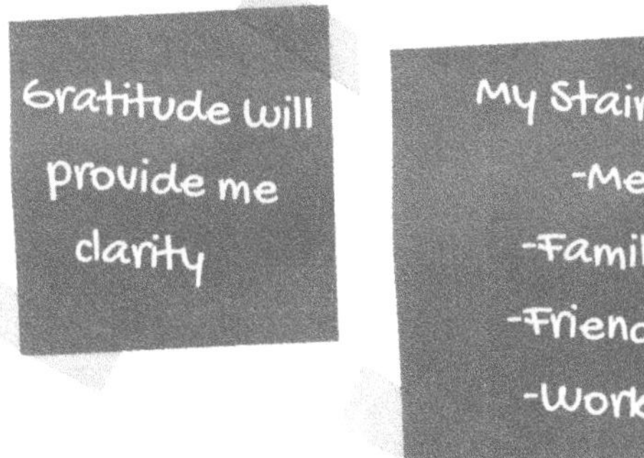

## The Shift: We're not walking in a circle
## We are on a spiral staircase

I realized that every time I came back to a familiar struggle, I had more clarity than the time before. I wasn't stuck; I was one level higher. I was leveling up! I realized the circle I thought I was walking was actually elevating; it was a spiral staircase.

When we stop fearing the return of obstacles, we can use the tools we have or have the awareness to find new ones, to bring us back to the present moment. Each time we revisit an area of life on our spiral staircase, we aren't the same person we were before.

WE are stronger, WE are more prepared, and WE are more present.

## My Tool: Imagining the Spiral Up

When I am hitting a major growth edge and feel that "circling," I take a moment to look at my spiral staircase. I look at the ways life is providing me exactly what I need, and sit in a moment of gratitude, which brings me back to the present moment.

## The Level Up

In what areas of your life do you feel stuck in a circle?

# MY SPIRAL STAIRCASE

# WHAT DOES YOUR SPIRAL STAIRCASE LOOK LIKE?

I invite you to think about what your spiral staircase looks like.

Can you see the subtle differences in how you are handling these areas in your life compared to a year ago?

# GROWTH EDGE 5
## INTENTIONAL TIME

I believe it is important to understand the role we play in the home. When I started shifting my frequency, my entire home shifted. Think of frequency here as the invisible lines that radiate out of us from our nervous system. When I started truly being intentional with my time, my nervous system began to shift. My frequency started to become more grounded and calm. It started with prioritizing myself and meeting my needs, which has overflowed through the entire house.

### The Shift: Our frequency leads the home

. Taking time for ourselves isn't selfish; it's the frequency shift our household needs.  When we start prioritizing ourselves, and our capacity for intentional time overflows into our families.

### Intentional time with myself: Prioritizing my nervous system

My goal is to become deeply aware of what my nervous system needs. I tune into finding time for myself, and no, a solo grocery trip does not count! I'm talking about doing things that actually bring me joy and help ground me.

## Intentional time in my marriage: Speaking each other's love languages

For us, intentional time means speaking each other's love languages. Mine (as defined by Dr. Gary Chapman) is Quality Time. My husband's is Acts of Service. Most days, our time looks like these intentional actions: I make his lunch before work, or we wake up before the kids to have screen-free time together before the day starts.

## Intentional time with my kids: Screen-free time

I prioritize 10 to 15 minutes with each child, doing exactly what they want to do. This time is no screens, no distractions, and 100% connection! It doesn't have to be grand gestures or money spent. This is a practice of prioritizing my time with my child. It is normal to have hard days finding the time or ability to connect. The more I find myself going back to the basics of prioritizing my nervous system, the more I find a greater capacity for screen free time with my kids. I am more grounded and more present. The frequency coming from my nervous system is calm and maybe even joyful at times!

**The Level Up**

When you start taking intentional time to prioritize your nervous system , your leading frequency in  the household shifts everywhere.

What is one non-negotiable thing you will do to regulate your nervous system?

# Growth Edge 6
## Small Clean Wins

I used to find myself  getting stuck in this never-ending down spiral of feeling exhausted by my to-do list. I was overwhelmed with the mess of my house, feeling like I was always playing catch up, while also feeling guilty because I was never present enough with my kids. After listening to a podcast talking about starting your day with a "small win." I decided to try starting my day with a "small clean win." For me, this meant making my bed.

I had thought about how the mess in the house really gets away from me quickly, and before I know it, I let it be the controlling factor on how present I am.

Now, I was going to start prioritizing a small clean win. It became sticky note worthy for me: "Make the bed." This signals to my nervous system that I don't have to let the overwhelm of the mess take control.

## The Shift: We deserve a clean environment

Making my bed has become a signal, a small win that creates a ripple effect through the house. I find balance in routine because I start my day with a small clean win.

We all have a different level for what feels "clean" and what feels "chaos". This growth edge isn't about striving for a perfectly clean environment all of the time. It's about being able to recognize your personal level of "clean" and being able to prioritize your small clean win. Helping you can show up more present and regulated.

## My Tool: The Future Self Gift

When the mess and the never-ending list start feeling overwhelming. I stop. I take a breath. Instead of looking at the task, I look towards my future self.

I feel how good it's going to feel for that future self, once that task is completed. Then I focus on one small clean win, and know how great it's going to feel when that task is completed.

### The Level Up

Maybe making your bed is that small clean win.
Maybe it's starting out by doing the dishes or tackling that pile of papers that has been sitting in the corner for weeks.
Whatever it is, remember this is a small win you're gifting the future you.
What "small clean win" can you claim today to show yourself that you deserve a clean environment?

# GROWTH EDGE 7
## CHOOSE YOUR HARD

My husband and I were talking about how heavy life can feel. It's easy to fall into the mindset that a "hard life" just happens to us. Then it clicked: we get to be active participants in our hard. We have the power to choose.

To be clear, I know that situations happen that are completely out of our control. I realize that while we can't always choose the situation, we can choose how we navigate through it. We have the power to focus on what we can control and decide which "hard" we want to dedicate our energy towards.

I see this constantly in parenthood.
- It's hard to stay in survival mode- to be burned out, constantly on edge, and passing negative patterns down to our kids.
- It's also hard to be present- to do the work on ourselves, to face our own "stuff", rewire our thoughts, and regulate our nervous systems so we don't pass down those unhelpful patterns.

Both are hard.

### The Shift: Choose Your Hard

"Choose Your Hard" has become one of our core family sayings.  This isn't about ignoring the pain of the things we can't control. It's about reclaiming our power in the areas we can control. When we look at our lives with clarity, we can ask: "Which hard am I willing to hold?"

### My Tool: I Have the Power to Choose

When I'm leveling up on my spiral staircase, I write "I have the power to choose" on a sticky note.  For example, if I am repeatedly hitting a growth edge in parenting, I remind myself that I have the power to choose how I show up. I look at the situation and ask which hard I want to hold. I choose the path of learning a new tool- speaking with intention and regulation, because I know where that path leads now.

### The Level Up

I invite you to look at a difficult moment in your parenting right now. You have the power to choose which version of "hard" you want to live. If the hard of survival mode is costing you too much, you have the power to choose the hard of healing. Becoming more aware of your own triggers. Gaining wisdom from these moments. It's not easy, but it will be yours. You have the power to choose.

I have the
power to
choose

# GROWTH EDGE 8
## THE REPAIR AND RESET

**This is the most important tool I have as a parent, because no one is perfect.** Even as I write this, I still have moments where I lose my shit! Just the other day, I was overstimulated to the max. I screamed right at my kids, and could see their scared and hurt feelings.

The guilt hit me so fast. I like to remind myself in these moments: "Guilt is a normal human response." Using my tool of repairing with myself first, I did not let that guilt downspiral into shame.

I like to use a mantra from Dr. Becky Kennedy to ground myself:  "I am a good parent who had a hard moment."
I remind myself  that I am learning right alongside my kids; I am learning that while all emotions are valid, not all behaviors are okay.

## The Shift: The Gift of Repair

This requires a level of connection that may not have been modeled to us as children. We might be creating what this looks and feels like for the first time in our homes. How amazing are we, modeling for our children something everyone deserves to experience in their life!

When we model repair with our children, this becomes their standard! So when they have hard moments, they will have a tool for repair with themselves and those around them.

## My Tool: The Three Rs

**Repair with myself first:** I start by reading my sticky note: "I am a good parent having a hard moment. I am still learning." I then move into somatic release- a physical movement like tapping, wringing a towel, or deep breathing. Moving the emotional energy out of my body. Finally, I sit with myself for a moment, checking with my nervous system, to make sure I am calm and ready to connect with my child. When the repair with our children comes from a grounded place, we get to model the connection that lives on the other side of that dysregulation.

**Repair with my kids:** Inspired by the work of Dr. Becky Kennedy, here is how I lead the repair with my children. "I am sorry I yelled. You didn't deserve to experience that. I was feeling (emotion) and took that out on you. I am working on how to stay calm, even when I am feeling (emotion). How are you feeling?" Then actively listen to my child and provide support to make them feel safe.

**Reset** : We find a way to laugh. Laughter turns the brain back on, pulling the body out of fight-or-flight and back into connection.

## The Level Up

The next time you need to repair, pause. Repair with yourself first.
Can you notice the connection you are giving to yourself and your child?

# Growth Edge 9
## Have Fun and Laugh

At some point along my journey,  I decided to stop waiting for "perfect" conditions to find joy. I started  choosing to laugh and have fun more. Here is my truth: I was in survival fog for so long that I actually forgot how to laugh. When I first heard of the idea of laughing more to improve my quality of life, it was forced.

 At first, I would stand in my kitchen and force myself to say "Ha, Ha, Ha." I would write it on a sticky note as a reminder! I would do it over and over again like a crazy person until it sounded so ridiculous that I actually started laughing. I had to start somewhere!

## The Shift: Finding Joy in the Little Things

As a homeschooling parent, I used to get lost in the hustle. I thought I couldn't have fun until the "to-do" list was checked off. Reality is- the list never ends.

Remember growth edge 6: we deserve a clean environment , but we also deserve a life that doesn't feel like a never-ending chore list. It's a balance. I have given myself permission to prioritize fun- whether that's singing while doing dishes, or having a random dance party in the living room.

## My Tool: Joy Reminder

When stress takes hold and laughter feels out of reach, I go back to my basics.

I write "Laugh More" and  "Find Joy in the Little Things" on a sticky note! Hang it up and give myself the visual reminder. I start focusing on the little funny things my kids say or do, and choose to make a big laugh out of it. This usually turns into a beautiful laughing session, and my entire house joins in.

## The Level Up

Finding joy or laughing can be hard or even awkward at first. Which hard are you willing to choose?

When was the last time you met your environment with joy?

# Growth Edge 10
## The Ever-Evolving Parent

**Being an Ever-Evolving Parent means that we will never be "done".** That's because we aren't projects that need to be finished; we are people who need to be nurtured.

There will be days when we hit those same growth edges again- the environment is messy,  we snap at our kids, and go back to the repair. There will be times when choosing our "hard" feels confusing or even impossible. In those moments, take a breath and know: **That is exactly where the growth happens.**

By choosing to be "Ever-Evolving," we are changing so much for our families. We are teaching our children that it's okay to be human and it's okay to make mistakes. We are modeling what it looks like to live with intention rather than just reacting to the world around us.

**The Level Up**

Our kids don't need a perfect parent; they need a present, ever-evolving one.
Welcome to the journey.
 We're doing it together.

## Let's Connect

**-Questions about the TRTP™ process?**
**-Ready for one-on-one coaching?**

I look forward to connecting with you.

**Email: Janowiaknikki@gmail.com**
**Instagram: @theeverevolvingmama**

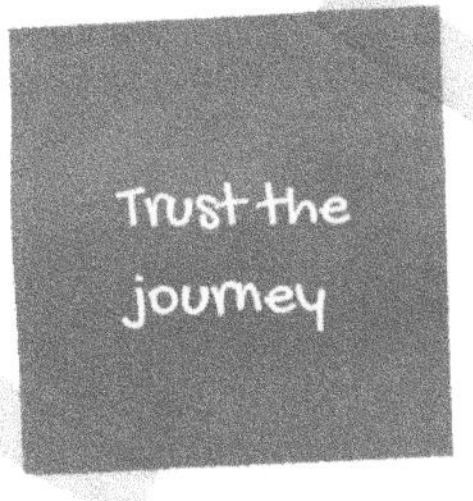

# Sticky Note
# Quick Guide

| Growth Edge | Old Way | New Way |
| --- | --- | --- |
| I am Responsible For My Healing | If everyone would just change I would be okay | Focus on what I can control |
| Foundational Work | I am always in survival mode | I am finding my way out of the fog |
| I Am What I Consume | My environment keeps me in survival mode | I create the environment around me to thrive |
| Spiral Staircase | I am walking in circle | I am ascending on a spiral staircase |
| Intentional Time | There is never enough time for me to think about my needs | It is important for me to prioritize my own time. My frequency leads the home |
| Small Clean Win | I am overwhelmed by the mess | I deserve a small win and a clean environment |
| Choose Your Hard | There's nothing I can do about my situation | I have the power to choose |
| The Repair and Rest | I am a bad parent | I am learning and it's safe to connect and repair with myself. I learn from my hard moments |
| Have Fun and Laugh | I can't even remember the last time I laughed | I find joy in the little things |
| Ever-Evolving Parent | I am stuck<br>I am failing | I am ever-evolving |

# My Favorite Resources

While the growth edges and concepts in this guide are born from my own evolution and my work supporting others, I am deeply grateful for the teachers and authors who provided a cleared path and shared language for the journey of presence and regulation. If you feel called to explore further, I highly recommend:

**Books & Authors**
- **Hold on to Your Kids-** Dr. Gabor Maté
- **The 5 Love Languages-** Dr. Gary Chapman
- **The 5 Love Languages of Children-** Dr. Gary Chapman
- **The Parenting Map-**Dr. Shefali Tsabary
- **Let Them Theory-**Mel Robbins
- **Awakened Family-** Dr. Shefali Tsabary
- **No Bad Parts-** Dr. Richard Schwartz
- **Breaking the Habit of Being Yourself**- Dr. Joe Dispenza
- **The Conscious Parent**-Dr. Shefali Tsabary

**Tools & Modalities**
- TRTP™ (The Richards Trauma Process)
- EFT (Emotional Freedom Technique)
- HeartMath®
- Somatic Regulation

**Podcasts**
- The Mel Robbins Podcast
- Dr. Becky Good Inside

# THANK YOU

To my Husband, Kyle, for always supporting every version of me. I am who I am today and who I will be tomorrow because we are such a great team.

To my children, Amara and Odysseus. You have become my greatest path to enlightenment.

To my amazing community of family and friends. Your support has given me the energy and time to continue to step into the future I am consciously creating.

To myself, I am so incredibly proud of the person you are today.

www.ingramcontent.com/pod-product-compliance
Lightning Source LLC
Chambersburg PA
CBHW041216150726
48006CB00016B/2280